CLA...
MAKING

A Thorough, Step-by-Step Guide to Fully Understanding, Learning, and Perfecting Homemade Crafts with Ease, Allowing You to Create Like a Professional Even if You Have No Previous Experience or Skills in Crafting

JULIANE KOHL

Copyright © 2025 By Juliane Kohl

All Right Reserved

No part of this book may be reproduced, stored in a retrieval system, or transmitted in any form—whether by electronic, mechanical, photocopying, recording, scanning, or any other means—without prior written permission from the author, except for brief excerpts used in reviews, scholarly analyses, or press commentary.

For permissions, licensing inquiries, or to submit a request, please contact the author in writing directly.

Published by Juliane Kohl

Disclaimer

This book is intended to provide general guidance and educational support for learning homemade craft-making techniques. While the methods and advice shared here may assist in skill development, they should not be considered a replacement for personalized instruction from an experienced craft expert. Individual results will vary depending on practice, experience, and adherence to proper techniques.

The author and publisher do not guarantee the completeness, reliability, or suitability of the material for every learner. Craft-making is ever-evolving, and this book may not reflect the most current methods, tools, or innovations. Always consult a skilled instructor to address your specific goals, challenges, or unique needs.

Safety and Responsibility

Proper use of tools, materials, and techniques is essential to avoid injury or damage. Follow safety guidelines provided by qualified instructors or craft experts.

The author and publisher disclaim all liability for any harm, loss, or damage—including to personal property, tools, or well-being—that may result from the use, misuse, or misinterpretation of this book's content. By engaging with this material, you assume full responsibility for your crafting journey and agree to prioritize safe, informed practices.

Table of Contents

What This Book Offers 9

CHAPTER ONE 13

Introduction to Clay Pottery Making 13

Understanding the Basics of Clay Pottery and Its Rich History 14

Overview of Different Types of Clay and Their Unique Properties..15

Key Tools and Materials You'll Need to Start Pottery Making 17

The Role of Creativity and Patience in Mastering Pottery Skills...20

Safety Precautions and Setting Up Your Workspace Effectively..21

CHAPTER TWO 25

Clay Preparation and Understanding Clay Types 25

Overview of Different Clay Types: Earthenware, Stoneware, Porcelain..25

How to Choose the Right Clay for Your Project ..27

Techniques for Wedging and Conditioning Clay .29

Moisture Content and Its Importance for Shaping Clay..30

Troubleshooting Common Clay Preparation Problems 32

5

CHAPTER THREE 35

Introduction to Wheel Throwing Techniques 35

Setting Up the Pottery Wheel for Beginners 36

Centering Clay on the Wheel – Tips for Mastering the Technique 37

Basic Steps to Throw a Simple Bowl or Cup 38

Common Mistakes in Wheel Throwing and How to Fix Them 39

Essential Tools for Wheel Throwing 40

CHAPTER FOUR 43

Hand Building Techniques for Pottery 43

1. Coil Building: Step-by-Step Guide for Beginners 44

2. Slab Building: Creating Pottery with Flat Clay Pieces 46

3. Pinch Pots: Simple, Beginner-Friendly Techniques 48

4. How to Use Molds for Hand-Building Pottery . 49

5. Creative Ideas for Adding Texture and Patterns to Hand-Built Pieces 51

CHAPTER FIVE 55

Kiln Firing Process and Tips for Beginners 55

Understanding the Purpose and Types of Kilns .. 56

Loading and Firing Your Kiln Safely 58

How to Manage Temperature Settings During Firing 59

Identifying and Solving Common Firing Problems 61

How to Choose the Right Firing Schedule for Your Project 63

CHAPTER SIX 65

Glazing Techniques and Finishing Touches in Clay Pottery Making... 65

Different Types of Glazes: Gloss, Matte, and Underglaze 66

Applying Glaze: Dipping, Brushing, and Pouring Techniques 67

How to Prevent Glazing Mistakes Like Pinholes, Crawling, and Crazing 69

Using Wax Resist and Layering Glaze for Creative Effects 70

Tips for Experimenting with Colors and Textures in Glazing 71

CHAPTER SEVEN 75

Common Concerns and FAQs in Pottery Making 75

How to Fix Cracking and Warping Issues in Clay . 75

What to Do When Clay Is Too Wet or Too Dry During Shaping 78

Best Practices for Maintaining and Cleaning Pottery Tools 80

What to Expect During Kiln Firing and Troubleshooting Underfired Pieces.....................82

FAQs: Understanding Glazes, Firing Schedules, and Safe Handling of Materials 84

THE END 87

What This Book Offers

Everything I Need to Know on Clay Pottery Making is an essential guide for both beginners and intermediate potters who are eager to master the art of pottery making. Pottery is not just a craft; it's an ancient art form that has been passed down through generations, and this book immerses you in the process while fostering your creativity and technical skills. With detailed insights, you'll learn the fundamentals of clay pottery while also developing the patience and precision needed to create stunning, hand-made pottery pieces.

This book begins with a comprehensive introduction, helping you understand the significance of clay pottery's rich history. It covers everything from the various types of clay and their properties to the tools and materials needed to get started. You'll discover how creativity and patience go hand-in-hand when it comes to mastering the craft, and you'll be guided through safety precautions to ensure a safe and effective workspace.

As you progress through the book, you'll dive into the world of clay preparation. Understanding the different types of clay—earthenware, stoneware, and porcelain—is crucial for selecting the right material for your projects. With easy-to-follow steps, you'll learn how to wedge and condition clay, ensuring its proper moisture content, and how to troubleshoot common issues. The book arms you with the knowledge you need to confidently approach clay preparation and avoid pitfalls.

For those new to wheel throwing, Everything I Need to Know on Clay Pottery Making provides a beginner-friendly introduction to wheel techniques. You'll explore the basics of setting up a pottery wheel, centering clay, and throwing simple shapes like bowls and cups. With practical advice and tips to correct common mistakes, this section ensures you'll quickly gain confidence in your wheel-throwing skills.

This book also covers hand-building techniques such as coil building, slab building, and pinch pots. These methods are perfect for those who prefer working with their hands over using a wheel. You'll also learn how to use molds and add unique textures and patterns to your pieces, encouraging you to explore your creativity while developing your skills.

Firing your pieces is a crucial step in pottery, and the book thoroughly explains the kiln firing process for beginners. You'll understand how to safely load and fire your kiln, manage temperatures, and troubleshoot issues like cracking and warping. Clear, concise instructions ensure you'll confidently handle the firing process, ensuring your work is durable and long-lasting.

Finally, the glazing techniques and finishing touches section will guide you in choosing the right glaze, applying it correctly, and experimenting with colors and textures.

With advice on avoiding glazing mistakes, you'll transform your pottery into beautifully finished works of art. Whether you're interested in glossy or matte finishes or more experimental techniques, this book provides the tools you need to perfect your pottery-making skills.

CHAPTER ONE

Introduction to Clay Pottery Making

Clay pottery has been a fundamental art form for centuries, dating back to the early civilizations of Mesopotamia and Ancient Egypt. It has evolved through the ages, from being a functional craft to a highly valued art form. Today, pottery is appreciated for its utility, artistic expression, and therapeutic qualities. This guide aims to take you on a comprehensive journey into the world of clay pottery making, whether you are a beginner or an enthusiast looking to deepen your understanding.

Pottery offers endless possibilities for creativity, from functional items like mugs and bowls to decorative sculptures and intricate designs. However, understanding the essential aspects of clay pottery will help you refine your craft and create beautiful, long-lasting pieces.

Understanding the Basics of Clay Pottery and Its Rich History

Clay pottery has a rich history that stretches across cultures and civilizations, each contributing unique techniques and styles. Early pottery was often hand-built, using the coil, pinch, or slab methods, and was primarily used for storage and cooking. Over time, wheel-throwing techniques were developed, allowing for more complex and symmetrical designs.

Ancient cultures such as the Greeks and Chinese have made significant contributions to pottery, including the use of glazes and the development of intricate patterns and motifs. Today, modern pottery continues to draw inspiration from these historical methods while incorporating new materials and tools.

Understanding the cultural significance of pottery and how it has shaped human history will deepen your appreciation for this timeless craft. You are not just making a functional item; you are participating in an ancient tradition that has evolved over millennia.

Overview of Different Types of Clay and Their Unique Properties

Choosing the right type of clay is critical to your pottery project. There are various types of clay, each with distinct characteristics that affect how they behave during the shaping, drying, and firing processes. Some of the most common types include:

1. Earthenware Clay: This is one of the most commonly used clays, especially for beginners. It is soft and easy to mold, making it ideal for hand-building projects. Earthenware is fired at a low temperature and results in a porous, rustic finish unless it is glazed. It is

widely used for decorative pottery and items like flowerpots.

2.   Stoneware Clay: Known for its durability and versatility, stoneware clay is fired at a higher temperature, making it more robust and waterproof without the need for glaze. It is often used for functional pieces such as dinnerware and mugs. Its medium plasticity makes it relatively easy to work with, and it is available in various textures and colors.

3.   Porcelain Clay: Porcelain is the finest and most delicate type of clay, often associated with high-end ceramics. It is fired at an extremely high temperature, resulting in a smooth, glass-like finish. Porcelain is harder to work with due to its low plasticity, but it is ideal for creating intricate, refined pieces like fine china and decorative sculptures.

4.   Ball Clay: This highly plastic clay is often added to other clays to increase workability. It is not typically used alone but serves as an important component in achieving the desired plasticity in certain mixtures.

5. Fire Clay: Fire clay can withstand high temperatures and is often used to make firebricks or as an ingredient in stoneware or porcelain blends. It's less plastic than other clays, so it's often combined with more malleable clays to achieve the desired texture.

Understanding the properties of each type of clay will allow you to select the right material for your project, ensuring that the final product meets your expectations in terms of durability, texture, and finish.

Key Tools and Materials You'll Need to Start Pottery Making

Starting pottery doesn't require a massive investment in tools, but having the right equipment will make the process smoother and more enjoyable. Here are the essential tools you will need:

1. Potter's Wheel: For those interested in wheel-throwing techniques, a potter's wheel is a must. It helps

create symmetrical and perfectly round pieces, which would be difficult to achieve by hand alone.

2. Clay: As discussed, selecting the appropriate clay for your project is crucial. Make sure to purchase clay that suits your intended project, whether it be earthenware, stoneware, or porcelain.

3. Work Surface: A sturdy, clean, and flat surface is essential for hand-building techniques. Consider using a worktable covered with canvas to prevent clay from sticking and to absorb moisture.

4. Clay Cutter and Wire Tool: These are used for cutting large chunks of clay and removing pots from the wheel without damaging the base.

5. Ribs and Scrapers: These flat tools help smooth and shape clay during the building process. They are available in metal, wood, or rubber, depending on the finish you want.

6. Needle Tool: This sharp tool is used for trimming, scoring, and creating fine details in your work. It's also useful for testing the thickness of your piece.

7. Loop and Ribbon Tools: These are great for carving and hollowing out clay, particularly for intricate designs or when reducing the thickness of your pot.

8. Sponges: A sponge helps to smooth your clay and can be used to add water while you're working on the wheel.

9. Kiln: A kiln is necessary to fire your pottery and make it durable. For beginners, consider looking into shared studio spaces that provide access to kilns, as they can be a significant investment.

With the right tools and materials, you'll be well-equipped to bring your pottery visions to life.

The Role of Creativity and Patience in Mastering Pottery Skills

Pottery is an art form that requires both creativity and patience. Each step in the process, from preparing the clay to firing the finished piece, demands attention to detail and a willingness to experiment. Creativity comes into play when designing your piece, whether you're shaping it by hand or using the potter's wheel. The possibilities are endless, from sleek and minimalist designs to intricate patterns and textures.

However, pottery also requires patience. There will be times when a piece cracks, collapses, or doesn't turn out as expected. Rather than becoming discouraged, use these moments as learning opportunities. The art of pottery is a journey, and each mistake brings you closer to mastering your craft.

The drying and firing stages of pottery also require patience, as rushing can lead to cracks or other imperfections. Take your time, enjoy the process, and allow your skills to develop naturally over time.

Safety Precautions and Setting Up Your Workspace Effectively

Before you begin working with clay, it's essential to set up a safe and organized workspace. Pottery can be messy, so it's best to designate a specific area for your craft. Here are some safety tips and workspace setup recommendations:

1. Ventilation: Ensure that your workspace is well-ventilated, especially if you are working with dry clay dust or glazes, which can contain harmful chemicals. Wear a dust mask when sanding or cleaning up dry clay.

2. Tools Organization: Keep your tools organized and within easy reach to avoid accidents or spills while

working. Invest in storage solutions like toolboxes, shelves, or pegboards to maintain a tidy workspace.

3. Cleanliness: Clean up your workspace regularly to prevent the buildup of clay dust, which can pose health risks when inhaled. Use wet cleaning methods (such as mopping or wiping with damp cloths) rather than sweeping, which can spread dust into the air.

4. Protective Clothing: Wear old clothes or an apron to protect yourself from getting dirty. Clay can stain, and some glazes can be harmful if they come into contact with your skin.

5. Kiln Safety: If you have your own kiln, make sure to follow the manufacturer's instructions and safety guidelines. Always fire the kiln in a well-ventilated area and keep a fire extinguisher nearby in case of emergencies.

By setting up your workspace with these safety measures in mind, you can focus on the creative aspects of pottery without worry.

Mastering the art of clay pottery making is a rewarding experience that offers both creative fulfillment and practical skills. By understanding the different types of clay, using the right tools, and practicing patience, you can create beautiful, functional, and decorative pieces that reflect your artistic vision.

CHAPTER TWO
Clay Preparation and Understanding Clay Types
Overview of Different Clay Types: Earthenware, Stoneware, Porcelain

The journey into clay pottery begins with understanding the different types of clay and how each behaves during the crafting process. There are three main categories of clay used in pottery: earthenware, stoneware, and porcelain. Each of these types has distinct characteristics that influence their workability, firing temperatures, and final appearance.

- Earthenware: This is one of the most common types of clay and has been used historically in pottery around the world. It is relatively soft and easy to shape, making it ideal for beginners. Earthenware is typically fired at a lower temperature, resulting in a porous and less durable product unless glazed. It is known for its warm, red-brown color after firing, but it is also available in white and buff varieties. Its plasticity makes it easy to mold, but it can crack if not handled carefully.

- Stoneware: Fired at higher temperatures than earthenware, stoneware is denser, stronger, and non-porous after firing. This makes it an excellent choice for functional pottery like mugs, plates, and bowls that need to hold liquids. Stoneware clay is often grey when wet and transforms into a light brown, buff, or greyish-white color after firing. It strikes a balance between the workability of earthenware and the strength of porcelain, making it versatile for a range of projects.

- Porcelain: Known for its fine, white, and smooth texture, porcelain is the most delicate and challenging type of clay to work with. It has very little plasticity, making it harder to shape and prone to collapsing if not carefully managed. However, it produces beautiful, high-quality, translucent pottery when fired at high temperatures. Porcelain is often used for decorative pieces and fine tableware. Its purity and smooth surface are favored by experienced potters who appreciate its ability to hold intricate details.

How to Choose the Right Clay for Your Project

Choosing the right clay for your project is a critical step in ensuring success in pottery making. Your choice will depend on the type of project, the final use of the piece, and your level of expertise.

- For beginners, earthenware is often the best choice because of its workability and forgiving nature. It's easier to shape, making it suitable for practice and creating decorative pieces such as vases, flower pots, or simple sculptures.

- Functional pottery like dinnerware, mugs, or cookware that will be exposed to liquids or heat requires a stronger and more durable clay, making stoneware the go-to option. Stoneware is less likely to chip or crack, ensuring the longevity of your creations.

- Experienced potters seeking to create fine, high-quality pieces such as figurines, artistic sculptures, or luxury dinnerware often turn to porcelain. Its ability to achieve thin, intricate designs and a smooth, glass-like finish makes it ideal for advanced projects.

Remember to also consider your kiln capabilities. Earthenware fires at lower temperatures, typically between 1,000°C to 1,150°C, while stoneware and porcelain need much higher temperatures, from 1,200°C to 1,400°C.

Techniques for Wedging and Conditioning Clay

Once you've selected the appropriate clay, proper preparation through wedging and conditioning is essential. This ensures that the clay is uniform, free of air bubbles, and ready for shaping.

• Wedging is similar to kneading dough in baking. It involves pressing the clay with your hands to remove air pockets, which can cause the piece to crack or explode in the kiln. Wedging also aligns the clay particles, making it more pliable and easier to work with. The two most common wedging techniques are the ram's head and spiral method.

o In the ram's head method, the clay is rolled into a large ball and pushed down with the palms of the hands, rotating the ball each time to keep the process consistent. The goal is to eliminate any air pockets.

o	The spiral method involves pushing the clay in a circular motion, folding it in on itself repeatedly. This technique is often used for larger batches of clay and ensures even distribution of moisture and particles.

•	Conditioning the clay is the next step. This involves allowing the wedged clay to sit for a period to stabilize its moisture content. If the clay is too dry or too wet, it can be difficult to shape, so conditioning helps achieve the perfect balance.

Moisture Content and Its Importance for Shaping Clay

The moisture content of your clay is one of the most critical factors in shaping and working with the material. Too much moisture can make the clay overly soft and weak, causing it to slump or collapse during shaping. On the other hand, clay that is too dry can be difficult to mold and may crack during the shaping process.

- When clay is too wet, it becomes sticky and hard to control, especially on the potter's wheel. If you notice your piece losing shape or sagging, it may need to be left to dry slightly before continuing. To do this, cover the piece with a damp cloth or plastic wrap to allow for slow drying.

- Too dry clay, on the other hand, will resist your efforts to shape it. This can be remedied by adding small amounts of water and kneading the clay thoroughly. Be careful not to add too much water, as this can quickly make the clay too wet again. Spraying the surface with a mist of water can help maintain a manageable moisture level as you work.

The goal is to maintain a balanced moisture content that allows you to mold and shape the clay effectively. The right amount of moisture ensures that the clay remains soft enough to work with while maintaining enough structural integrity to hold its shape.

Troubleshooting Common Clay Preparation Problems

During the clay preparation process, several issues can arise. Understanding these common problems and how to troubleshoot them will help prevent frustration and wasted material.

• Air bubbles: Air bubbles trapped in the clay are one of the most common problems, especially for beginners. If left in the clay, these bubbles can expand in the kiln, causing the piece to crack or even explode. To fix this, thorough wedging is crucial. Make sure to wedge the clay until no visible air pockets remain.

• Uneven moisture content: Sometimes, parts of the clay may be too dry while other parts are too wet. This often happens if the clay hasn't been properly conditioned. To fix this, knead the clay to redistribute the moisture. If necessary, add a small amount of water and knead again until the moisture is even throughout.

- Cracking: If your clay cracks during shaping, it may be too dry or not wedged properly. To prevent this, ensure that the clay is at the correct moisture level and free of air bubbles. You can also lightly spray the surface with water to restore flexibility as you work.

- Sticky clay: If your clay feels too sticky and adheres to your hands or tools, it likely has too much moisture. Let the clay sit out for a while, uncovered, to allow some of the moisture to evaporate. Alternatively, lightly dust your hands and tools with cornstarch to reduce the stickiness while shaping.

By preparing your clay with care and attention to detail, you set the foundation for a successful pottery-making process. The next steps, from shaping and throwing to firing and glazing, all depend on the quality of your clay preparation. Mastering these techniques early on will make the rest of the pottery process smoother and more enjoyable.

CHAPTER THREE
Introduction to Wheel Throwing Techniques

Wheel throwing is one of the most captivating and fundamental techniques in the world of pottery. Whether you're a beginner or a seasoned artisan, the process of shaping clay on a spinning wheel offers endless possibilities for creativity and personal expression. However, for beginners, the journey from a lump of clay to a beautiful, functional piece can seem challenging. Mastering wheel throwing requires patience, practice, and a thorough understanding of the essential techniques and tools. In this comprehensive guide, we'll explore the art of wheel throwing from setting up your wheel to perfecting your techniques, ensuring you're equipped with the knowledge to start your pottery-making journey.

Setting Up the Pottery Wheel for Beginners

Before you begin wheel throwing, setting up your pottery wheel correctly is crucial for comfort, safety, and success. Start by ensuring that the wheel is positioned on a sturdy surface at the correct height for your body. Your chair should allow your thighs to be parallel to the floor when your feet rest on the foot pedals. This helps maintain balance and reduce strain on your back.

Make sure you have adequate lighting and enough space around the wheel to move freely. Position your clay, tools, and water bucket within arm's reach, so you don't have to stop the wheel to reach for them. For beginners, an electric wheel is often preferred due to its consistent speed, but manual kick wheels can offer a more traditional experience. Ensure that your wheel's speed is adjustable, allowing you to slow it down as you learn and gradually increase as you gain confidence.

Centering Clay on the Wheel – Tips for Mastering the Technique

One of the most crucial and often challenging steps in wheel throwing is centering the clay. If your clay isn't properly centered, it will wobble and make it difficult to shape your piece. To begin, prepare a small lump of clay, approximately the size of a grapefruit, and wedge it to remove any air bubbles.

Start by slapping the clay onto the center of the wheel with enough force to make it stick firmly. Wet your hands and apply pressure with both palms as the wheel spins slowly. Lean in with your whole body, keeping your elbows close to your body for stability. Use your dominant hand to guide the clay upwards while using the other hand to push it down, creating a cone shape. Then, press it back down to a compact, centered form.

The key to centering is to focus on your body's movement rather than just your hands. Ensure that the speed of the wheel is fast enough to make the clay move but not so fast that it becomes unmanageable. Practice is essential—centering may take time to master, but it forms the foundation of every wheel-thrown piece.

Basic Steps to Throw a Simple Bowl or Cup

Once your clay is centered, you can begin the process of shaping your first piece. Start by using your thumbs to create an opening in the center of the clay. Slowly push down into the clay, keeping the wheel at a moderate speed, until you reach the desired depth, leaving enough clay at the base to create a sturdy bottom.

Next, use your fingers to widen the opening by pulling the walls outward for a bowl or upward for a cup. Make sure to work with even pressure, using both hands to guide the shape. Keep the walls of the piece consistent in thickness as you move your hands upwards, using the inside hand to support the shape while the outside hand gently pulls the clay.

As you form your piece, regularly wet your hands and the clay to keep everything smooth and prevent cracking. Once you've achieved the desired shape, you can use a rib tool to smooth the surface and a needle tool to trim any excess clay at the base.

Common Mistakes in Wheel Throwing and How to Fix Them

As with any new skill, mistakes are an inevitable part of the learning process. In wheel throwing, some common mistakes can make it difficult to create clean, even shapes. One frequent issue is uneven thickness in the walls of your piece, which can cause it to collapse. To avoid this, always use consistent pressure and regularly check the thickness as you work.

Another common mistake is wobbling clay, which often occurs when the clay isn't properly centered. If this happens, stop and recenter your clay before continuing. Additionally, beginners often struggle with speed control. If the wheel is spinning too fast, it can cause the clay to spiral out of control. Start slow and gradually increase the speed as needed.

A piece that is too wet can also cause problems, as excess water weakens the clay. Use a sponge to absorb any extra water from the surface, and be mindful of how often you wet your hands.

Essential Tools for Wheel Throwing

Having the right tools at hand can greatly enhance your wheel throwing experience. While the pottery wheel and clay are the main essentials, there are a few other key tools that will help you refine your technique and create more polished pieces:

- Rib Tool: Used for shaping and smoothing the surface of the clay. Ribs come in a variety of materials like wood, metal, and rubber.

- Needle Tool: Ideal for trimming excess clay, creating surface designs, and testing the thickness of your piece.

- Wooden Modeling Tool: A versatile tool that can be used for trimming, shaping, and smoothing the clay's surface.

- Sponge: Useful for keeping your hands and the clay moist as you work. A wet sponge can also be used to smooth out the surface of your piece.

- Cutting Wire: Used to slice clay and remove finished pieces from the wheel. The wire is typically stretched between two wooden handles for ease of use.

- Bat: A removable flat surface that sits on top of the wheel. Bats are especially useful for removing pieces from the wheel without distorting their shape.

By becoming familiar with these tools and incorporating them into your practice, you'll be able to refine your wheel throwing skills and create more consistent, professional-quality pieces.

With practice, patience, and the right approach, wheel throwing can be a deeply rewarding aspect of pottery making. Whether you're creating simple bowls or more complex forms, mastering these techniques will set the foundation for endless creativity in clay pottery.

CHAPTER FOUR

Hand Building Techniques for Pottery

Hand-building is one of the most accessible and creative methods for making pottery. It allows beginners to explore their artistic potential without the need for a pottery wheel, offering endless opportunities to shape and personalize clay pieces by hand. Below, we explore five essential hand-building techniques, providing detailed explanations and step-by-step instructions for coil building, slab building, pinch pots, using molds, and adding texture and patterns to your creations.

1. Coil Building: Step-by-Step Guide for Beginners

Coil building is one of the oldest and most versatile pottery techniques. It involves rolling out long, snake-like coils of clay and stacking them to build the walls of your pottery piece. This method offers tremendous flexibility in creating forms, from simple bowls to intricate vases and sculptures.

Step-by-Step Process:

1.	Prepare the Clay: Begin by kneading your clay to remove any air bubbles and ensure it's pliable. This process, known as wedging, is crucial to avoid cracks during firing.

2.	Roll the Coils: Take a small piece of clay and roll it into a long, even coil. Your coil should be about the thickness of a pencil, though you can vary the thickness depending on the size and shape of your project.

3. Create the Base: Start by shaping a flat disc of clay that will serve as the base for your pottery. You can either hand-shape this disc or cut it from a slab using a circular template.

4. Stack the Coils: Gently place the first coil around the outer edge of the base. Press down lightly to secure it. As you stack more coils, smooth the inside and outside of the walls with your fingers or a wooden tool to bond the coils together.

5. Shape Your Piece: You can manipulate the shape of your piece as you go, creating straight or curved walls, adding bulges, or even tapering the top for a unique design.

6. Refine and Smooth: Once you've reached the desired height, use your fingers, sponge, or a rib tool to smooth out any seams or bumps.

Coil building is an incredibly forgiving technique that allows you to go back and correct mistakes. It also encourages experimentation, so don't be afraid to try different shapes and patterns as you master the process.

2. Slab Building: Creating Pottery with Flat Clay Pieces

Slab building involves rolling out flat pieces of clay and cutting or shaping them to form the components of your pottery. This technique is ideal for creating geometric or architectural forms, such as boxes, trays, or plates.

Steps to Follow:

1. Prepare the Clay Slab: Begin by rolling out a slab of clay using a rolling pin or slab roller. The thickness of the slab should be uniform and typically about 1/4 inch, though this can vary depending on the project.

2. Cut the Shapes: Using a sharp knife or a clay cutter, cut out the shapes you need for your project. For

example, if you're building a box, you'll need four walls, a base, and potentially a lid.

3. Score and Slip: Before joining the pieces, score the edges that will be joined by scratching the surface lightly with a needle tool. Then, apply slip (a mixture of clay and water) to these scored areas to act as glue.

4. Join the Pieces: Press the edges together firmly, ensuring they are well-bonded. Use a wooden tool or your fingers to smooth the seams inside and outside the piece.

5. Refine and Decorate: Once the structure is complete, you can add additional elements, such as handles, feet, or decorative details, using extra slabs of clay.

Slab building opens the door to more structured forms and architectural shapes. It's an excellent technique for those looking to create pottery with clean lines or flat surfaces.

3. Pinch Pots: Simple, Beginner-Friendly Techniques

Pinch pots are one of the simplest and most satisfying techniques for hand-building pottery. This method involves pinching and shaping a small ball of clay into a pot with your fingers.

How to Make a Pinch Pot:

1. Start with a Ball of Clay: Begin by rolling a ball of clay in your hands. The size of the ball will determine the size of the finished pot, so start small if you're a beginner.

2. Create the Initial Opening: Use your thumb to press into the center of the ball, making a small well. Don't press too deep—about halfway is enough.

3. Pinch and Shape the Walls: Use your thumb inside the pot and your fingers on the outside to gently pinch and turn the clay. Work your way around the pot,

evenly pinching the walls until they are the desired thickness—typically about 1/4 inch.

4. Smooth and Refine: After shaping the pot, use a damp sponge to smooth the surface and refine the edges. You can leave the pot with a rustic, hand-made texture or smooth it completely for a polished look.

Pinch pots are an excellent introduction to pottery, allowing you to feel the clay in your hands and create organic, freeform shapes with minimal tools.

4. How to Use Molds for Hand-Building Pottery

Molds are a great tool for creating consistent shapes in hand-built pottery. They can be made from plaster, wood, or even everyday objects like bowls and plates.

Using Molds:

1. Prepare the Mold: Whether you're using a plaster mold or an everyday object, make sure it's clean and dry before use. For plaster molds, you may want to dust them with cornstarch to prevent sticking.

2. Roll Out a Slab: Roll out a slab of clay to a uniform thickness. This slab will be pressed into the mold to take its shape.

3. Press the Clay Into the Mold: Gently press the slab of clay into the mold, ensuring it conforms to the shape of the mold. Use a sponge or your fingers to press the clay into any crevices or corners.

4. Trim the Edges: Once the clay has been pressed into the mold, use a knife to trim away any excess clay from the edges.

5. Remove the Clay from the Mold: Allow the clay to firm up slightly (this is called "leather-hard" stage) before gently removing it from the mold. The clay should hold its shape but still be workable for additional shaping or decorating.

Molds are ideal for creating uniform bowls, plates, or cups and can save time when producing multiple pieces with the same design.

5. Creative Ideas for Adding Texture and Patterns to Hand-Built Pieces

Adding texture and patterns is where hand-building pottery becomes truly creative. There are endless ways to enhance your pottery with designs that reflect your personal style.

Ideas for Adding Texture:

1. Textured Tools: Use simple tools like forks, combs, or toothbrushes to create lines, dots, or cross-hatch patterns on your clay. Wooden or rubber stamps can also be pressed into the clay for intricate designs.

2. Natural Impressions: Press leaves, flowers, or other natural objects into the clay to create organic textures. These impressions will leave behind a detailed, natural pattern.

3. Carving and Incising: Once your piece reaches the leather-hard stage, you can carve into the surface using a needle tool or carving tools. Incising allows you to create intricate designs, such as geometric patterns or freeform drawings, directly on the clay.

4. Adding Slips and Underglazes: Another way to add visual interest is by applying colored slips or underglazes to the surface of your piece before firing. You can paint, stencil, or sponge on these decorative elements to create depth and dimension.

5. Combining Techniques: Don't be afraid to mix and match different methods for unique results. For instance, you might use stamps to create a border around a hand-carved central motif or apply a natural texture over a painted design.

Textures and patterns are a fantastic way to bring life to your pottery, and the possibilities are as limitless as your imagination.

By mastering these essential hand-building techniques—coil building, slab building, pinch pots, using molds, and adding creative textures and patterns—you'll be well on your way to crafting beautiful and unique clay pottery.

Whether you're a beginner or an experienced potter, these methods offer a world of possibilities to explore.

CHAPTER FIVE

Kiln Firing Process and Tips for Beginners

Firing pottery in a kiln is a crucial step in pottery making that transforms your soft, malleable clay pieces into durable ceramic works of art. For beginners, understanding the kiln firing process and how to manage it properly can seem overwhelming. However, with the right guidance and practice, you can master this essential aspect of pottery. This guide explores the purpose and types of kilns, the safe loading and firing process, temperature management, troubleshooting common firing problems, and how to choose the right firing schedule for your project.

Understanding the Purpose and Types of Kilns

What is a Kiln?

A kiln is a high-temperature oven or furnace used to fire clay pieces, permanently hardening them through a process known as vitrification. The heat from the kiln removes moisture from the clay and allows glazes to melt and bond to the surface, resulting in a durable and finished piece. Without firing, your pottery would remain fragile and easily broken.

Types of Kilns

When starting your pottery journey, it's essential to understand the different types of kilns available. Each type serves different needs, and choosing the right one for your work is vital.

1. Electric Kilns: These are the most common kilns for beginner and hobby potters. Electric kilns are easy

to use, affordable, and ideal for firing smaller pieces. They allow for precise control over temperature and firing schedules, which is important for ensuring consistent results.

2. Gas Kilns: Gas kilns use natural gas or propane as fuel and are often used by more experienced potters. They allow for better control over the atmosphere inside the kiln, which can influence the final appearance of the pottery, especially glazes. However, gas kilns require more maintenance and knowledge compared to electric ones.

3. Wood-Fired Kilns: These traditional kilns use wood as fuel and produce unique results due to the ash and flames interacting with the pottery. However, they require constant attention and skill to maintain consistent heat, making them less suited for beginners.

4. Raku Kilns: Raku kilns are small, typically gas-fired kilns used for rapid firing and cooling. Raku firing involves removing the pieces while still glowing hot, often producing dramatic and unpredictable glaze

effects. This type of kiln is popular for artistic experimentation but is not ideal for functional pottery.

Loading and Firing Your Kiln Safely

Preparing Your Pottery for Firing

Before loading your kiln, ensure that your pieces are completely dry, as any remaining moisture can cause them to crack or explode during firing. This drying process, known as bone-dry, should be done slowly and evenly. Ensure that your pieces are free of any trapped air pockets, which can also lead to breakage.

Loading the Kiln

Loading your kiln properly is key to successful firing. Always arrange your pottery so that air can circulate freely around each piece, as uneven heating can cause issues such as warping or cracking. Use kiln shelves and stilts to stack multiple layers of pottery, but ensure that none of the pieces touch, especially if they are glazed.

If glazed pieces touch during firing, they will fuse together permanently.

Safety Considerations

Kilns reach extremely high temperatures, so safety is a priority. Always ensure your kiln is in a well-ventilated space, as firing can release fumes that may be harmful. Never open the kiln while it's firing or immediately after, as the temperature inside can exceed 1000°F. Allow the kiln to cool completely before unloading to avoid thermal shock, which can cause your pieces to crack.

How to Manage Temperature Settings During Firing

The Importance of Temperature Control

Managing the temperature of your kiln is essential for achieving the desired results with your pottery. Most kilns allow you to set and control the temperature through built-in controllers or manual adjustments. The firing temperature will depend on the type of clay and glaze you are using.

There are two main stages of firing:

1. Bisque Firing: This is the first firing, which removes all moisture from the clay and turns it into a porous yet solid ceramic state. Bisque firing temperatures typically range from 1800°F to 1940°F (Cone 06 to Cone 04).

2. Glaze Firing: After bisque firing, your pieces are glazed and fired again. This second firing melts the glaze, bonding it to the pottery. Glaze firing temperatures vary depending on the glaze type but are usually higher than bisque firing, ranging from 2160°F to 2340°F (Cone 5 to Cone 10).

Firing Schedules and Ramps

When firing your kiln, the temperature should be increased gradually to prevent sudden thermal shock to your pottery. This gradual increase is known as ramping. A typical firing schedule includes three phases:

1. Ramp 1 (Slow Heat-Up): Slowly raise the temperature to around 500°F to allow moisture to evaporate gently. Heating too quickly in this stage can cause the clay to crack.

2. Ramp 2 (Moderate Heat-Up): Increase the temperature steadily to the desired bisque or glaze temperature. This is the stage where the clay starts to harden or the glaze begins to melt.

3. Ramp 3 (Cool-Down): After reaching the peak temperature, the kiln should cool slowly to avoid thermal shock. Never open the kiln until the temperature has dropped to below 200°F.

Identifying and Solving Common Firing Problems

Cracking

One of the most common problems beginners face is cracking during firing. This can be caused by improper drying, trapped air pockets, or firing the kiln too quickly. To prevent cracking, ensure your pieces are thoroughly dry before firing and follow a slow, steady heating process.

Warping

Warping occurs when a piece bends or distorts during firing. This can result from uneven heat distribution in the kiln or improper clay preparation. Ensure your kiln is loaded properly, and that pieces are of consistent thickness. If possible, place flat pieces (like plates) on kiln shelves for even support.

Glaze Defects

Glaze issues such as crazing (cracking of the glaze surface) or blistering (bubbles in the glaze) can be frustrating. These problems often occur due to improper glaze application or firing temperatures. To solve these issues, ensure you are applying the glaze evenly and following the recommended firing temperature for the specific glaze.

How to Choose the Right Firing Schedule for Your Project

Choosing the right firing schedule depends on the type of clay and glaze you are working with, as well as the size and thickness of your pieces. Each project may require slight adjustments to ensure the best results.

Factors to Consider:

1. Type of Clay: Low-fire clay (earthenware) typically fires at lower temperatures, while stoneware and porcelain require higher firing temperatures. Always refer to the manufacturer's recommendations for firing temperatures.

2. Type of Glaze: Different glazes require specific temperatures to mature. Low-fire glazes are typically used for earthenware, while high-fire glazes are suited

for stoneware and porcelain. Ensure your firing schedule matches both your clay and glaze.

3. Size and Thickness: Larger and thicker pieces require longer firing times to ensure even heat distribution. It's often recommended to fire larger pieces at a slower rate to prevent cracking or warping.

4. Desired Finish: If you're seeking a specific finish, such as a glossy or matte surface, your firing schedule can affect the result. For instance, a longer soak time (holding the kiln at the peak temperature) may enhance the glossiness of a glaze.

By understanding the kiln firing process, managing temperature settings, and troubleshooting common issues, you can create beautiful, durable pottery. While mastering kiln firing takes practice, starting with the right knowledge will ensure you achieve consistent and successful results with your clay creations.

CHAPTER SIX
Glazing Techniques and Finishing Touches in Clay Pottery Making

One of the most exciting aspects of pottery making is the glazing and finishing process. After shaping and firing your pottery, glazing allows you to bring your creation to life with color, texture, and a protective coating. Whether you're aiming for a glossy sheen, a matte surface, or an artistic layered effect, understanding the fundamentals of glazing will elevate your pottery to a new level of craftsmanship. Let's dive into the various techniques, types of glazes, and tips for achieving stunning results.

Different Types of Glazes: Gloss, Matte, and Underglaze

When it comes to glazing, the first step is to understand the different types of glazes available. Each glaze has its own unique characteristics that affect the final appearance of your pottery.

1. Gloss Glazes: Gloss glazes create a shiny, reflective surface that enhances the vibrancy of colors. They are often used on functional pieces like bowls, plates, and cups because they create a smooth, easy-to-clean finish. Gloss glazes tend to highlight every curve and detail of the pottery, making them perfect for pieces with intricate designs.

2. Matte Glazes: Matte glazes offer a smooth, non-reflective finish. Unlike gloss glazes, matte finishes provide a more subdued, sophisticated look. Matte glazes are excellent for artistic and decorative pieces where a muted, softer appearance is desired. They also

tend to emphasize texture, making them ideal for showcasing the raw beauty of clay.

3. Underglaze: Underglazes are applied before the clear glaze and are used to create detailed patterns or images on the surface of your pottery. They can be painted, sprayed, or drawn onto the pottery, providing a more controlled and precise decoration. After applying the underglaze, a clear or tinted glaze is applied over it to seal and protect the design.

Applying Glaze: Dipping, Brushing, and Pouring Techniques

The method of applying glaze to your pottery will greatly influence the final look. There are three main techniques for glaze application: dipping, brushing, and pouring.

1. Dipping: Dipping is one of the most efficient ways to apply glaze, especially for larger pieces. In this technique, the entire piece is dipped into a bucket of

glaze for a few seconds, ensuring an even and uniform coat. Potters often dip their pieces in different glazes to create layered effects or use wax resist to create intricate patterns.

2. Brushing: Brushing glaze onto your pottery allows for more control and customization. This technique is ideal for applying multiple colors, painting specific designs, or glazing smaller, detailed areas. Multiple coats are usually needed to achieve an even, opaque finish. It's important to use a soft, wide brush to avoid visible brush strokes on the final piece.

3. Pouring: Pouring glaze involves slowly pouring glaze over the surface of your pottery, creating natural, flowing patterns as the glaze drips down. This method is especially useful for larger pieces where dipping is impractical. Pouring can produce beautiful, organic effects, but care must be taken to ensure even coverage.

How to Prevent Glazing Mistakes Like Pinholes, Crawling, and Crazing

Glazing pottery can be a delicate process, and several common mistakes can arise if proper care isn't taken. Understanding these issues and how to prevent them can save your work from being ruined.

1. Pinholes: Pinholes are tiny holes that appear in the glaze after firing, often caused by trapped gases escaping from the clay. To prevent pinholes, ensure that your pottery is thoroughly cleaned and free of dust before glazing. Applying a thinner coat of glaze can also reduce the likelihood of pinholes forming.

2. Crawling: Crawling occurs when the glaze pulls away from the surface of the pottery, leaving bare patches. This is often caused by applying the glaze too thickly or by dust or grease on the pottery surface. To avoid crawling, make sure your pottery is clean and dry before glazing, and apply thin, even coats of glaze.

3. Crazing: Crazing refers to fine cracks that appear in the glaze after firing, often caused by a mismatch between the glaze and the clay body's shrinkage rates. To prevent crazing, select a glaze that is compatible with your clay body, and fire the piece at the correct temperature. Sometimes, adding more silica to the glaze can help reduce crazing.

Using Wax Resist and Layering Glaze for Creative Effects

Wax resist is a technique used to prevent glaze from adhering to certain areas of the pottery, creating a design or pattern. It involves applying wax to the pottery before glazing. The wax acts as a barrier, and once fired, the areas covered in wax remain unglazed, revealing the clay beneath. This technique is ideal for creating intricate designs, lines, or patterns.

Layering Glazes: Combining different glazes can produce stunning, multi-dimensional effects. For example, applying a matte glaze over a glossy one can create a unique contrast in texture and appearance. Layering different colors of glaze also allows for creative blending, as the glazes will melt and interact with each other during firing. Experimenting with glaze layering can lead to surprising and beautiful results, but it's important to test small samples before glazing an entire piece.

Tips for Experimenting with Colors and Textures in Glazing

One of the joys of pottery glazing is the ability to experiment with endless combinations of colors and textures. Here are a few tips to help you get started with creative glazing:

1. Test Tiles: Always create test tiles when experimenting with new glaze combinations. This will allow you to see how different glazes interact with each other and with your specific clay body. It's a small

investment of time that can prevent disappointment later.

2. Layering Colors: Try layering multiple colors of glaze to achieve depth and complexity in your pottery. For example, apply a lighter base color, then use a contrasting glaze for accents or details. The firing process will cause the colors to blend, creating unique visual effects.

3. Texture Enhancements: Use glaze to highlight the textures you've created in your pottery. Matte glazes often emphasize the natural texture of the clay, while gloss glazes can create a smoother, more polished finish. Experiment with different glazes to find what best complements the texture of your work.

4. Experiment with Thickness: The thickness of your glaze application can dramatically affect the final look of your pottery. Thicker glazes tend to create richer, more intense colors, while thinner coats can result in a more translucent or washed-out appearance.

Don't be afraid to experiment with different thicknesses to achieve the desired effect.

Mastering glazing techniques is key to creating beautiful, finished pottery pieces. By understanding the various types of glazes, perfecting your application methods, and avoiding common mistakes, you can achieve stunning results. Don't hesitate to experiment with different colors, textures, and effects to create truly unique and artistic pieces.

CHAPTER SEVEN

Common Concerns and FAQs in Pottery Making

Pottery making can be an incredibly rewarding and therapeutic art form, but like all creative processes, it comes with its own set of challenges and frequently asked questions. This section will address common concerns pottery enthusiasts often face, provide solutions to technical issues, and offer practical advice to help you improve your skills.

How to Fix Cracking and Warping Issues in Clay

Cracking and warping are two of the most frustrating issues potters face, especially during the drying and firing stages. These problems can happen due to various factors, including uneven drying, improper wedging, or incorrect moisture levels in the clay. Let's explore some ways to prevent and fix these problems.

1.   Preventing Cracks:

Cracks typically form when clay dries too quickly, especially in areas that are thinner than others. To avoid this, try to dry your pieces slowly and cover them loosely with plastic while they dry. If you notice cracks beginning to form during the drying process, use a damp sponge or slip (a liquid mixture of clay and water) to smooth them out before they get worse.

2.   Fixing Cracks After They Form:

If you notice cracks during shaping or after the piece has dried, gently moisten the area with a little water, then use clay slip to fill in the crack. After filling the crack, carefully smooth it over with your fingers or a flexible rib tool. For deeper cracks, you may need to press clay into the crack and reshape that section of the piece before smoothing it out.

3.   Dealing with Warping:

Warping happens when parts of the pottery dry at different rates or when the piece is too thin in certain areas. To avoid this, make sure your clay is wedged properly to remove any air bubbles and to evenly distribute moisture. Also, consider flipping the piece occasionally during the drying process to ensure even exposure to air. If warping occurs, you may have to reshape the piece while it's still somewhat malleable or trim the warped area to restore symmetry.

4.   Clay Body and Consistency:

Different clay bodies (types of clay) respond differently to drying, so choosing a consistent clay body for your project is essential. Try using clays with good plasticity and durability to reduce the risk of cracking and warping. Additionally, maintain the right moisture level by kneading and wedging your clay properly, ensuring it is not too wet or too dry.

What to Do When Clay Is Too Wet or Too Dry During Shaping

One of the most common issues during pottery shaping is dealing with clay that is either too wet or too dry. Each situation requires different handling techniques to ensure the best results.

1. Dealing with Wet Clay:

If your clay is too wet and sticky, it can be difficult to shape properly, as it will tend to sag and lose form. To fix this, try to let the clay air dry for a short while by leaving it uncovered. If it's still too wet after this, you can gently knead in some dry clay or let it sit on a porous surface (like a plaster slab) to absorb some moisture. Be cautious when working with very wet clay because it is more prone to warping and cracking during drying and firing.

2. Correcting Dry Clay:

On the other hand, if your clay is too dry and crumbly, you can attempt to rehydrate it by wrapping it in a damp cloth and sealing it in a plastic bag for several hours. This will allow the clay to absorb moisture evenly. If the clay is too dry to shape but not fully hardened, use a spray bottle to mist the surface while you work. However, once clay becomes completely bone dry, it cannot be rehydrated effectively for shaping and must be recycled or discarded.

3.   Managing Moisture During Work:

To prevent clay from drying out too quickly while you work, frequently mist your piece with water or use a damp sponge to keep the surface pliable. Keep a spray bottle handy to help control moisture levels and work in a cool, shaded environment to slow down the drying process.

Best Practices for Maintaining and Cleaning Pottery Tools

Taking care of your pottery tools is essential for ensuring their longevity and performance. Well-maintained tools can make a significant difference in the quality of your work, so it's important to establish good habits when cleaning and storing them.

1. Cleaning Tools After Each Session:

After every pottery session, thoroughly clean your tools by washing them in warm water. Use a soft sponge or cloth to remove any clay residue. Tools like wooden ribs and trimming tools can become dull if clay is left on them for too long, so avoid letting clay dry on the surface of your tools. Metal tools can rust if they remain wet for too long, so dry them immediately after washing.

2. Storing Tools Properly:

Store your tools in a dry place where they won't be exposed to moisture or extreme temperatures. Wooden tools should be kept in a cool area to prevent cracking, while metal tools should be stored in an airtight container to avoid rust. Grouping similar tools together can also make your workspace more organized and efficient.

3. Sharpening and Repairing Tools:

Over time, trimming and shaping tools may become dull. You can sharpen metal tools using a sharpening stone or fine-grit sandpaper. For wooden tools, consider sanding the edges to smooth out any nicks or rough areas that might form after extended use. Taking care of your tools means fewer interruptions in your creative process.

4. Specific Tool Maintenance Tips:

o Pottery wheels: Keep them clean and free of debris by wiping them down after each use. Ensure that bearings and belts are regularly checked for wear.

o	Sculpting tools: These often have intricate shapes that can trap clay, so pay extra attention when cleaning and dry them thoroughly.

o	Sponges: Clean sponges regularly to prevent bacteria buildup and replace them as needed.

What to Expect During Kiln Firing and Troubleshooting Underfired Pieces

Kiln firing is one of the most exciting, yet nerve-wracking, stages of pottery making. The firing process can dramatically alter your piece's appearance, strength, and functionality. However, things don't always go as planned, and it's important to know what to expect and how to troubleshoot common issues.

1.	The Firing Process Explained:

Kiln firing happens in two stages: bisque firing and glaze firing. Bisque firing removes moisture from the clay and hardens it, making the piece more durable for glazing. Glaze firing, on the other hand, fuses the glaze onto the pottery's surface, giving it a glossy, waterproof finish.

2. Underfired Pieces:

Underfired pottery can occur if the kiln doesn't reach the correct temperature or if the firing schedule is too short. When a piece is underfired, it may feel chalky, fragile, or have uneven glaze application. In this case, you can refire the piece, ensuring that the kiln reaches the appropriate temperature for the clay body and glaze you're using. Be sure to check your kiln's thermocouple and controls to ensure they are functioning correctly.

3. Firing Schedules and Temperature:

Each type of clay and glaze has its own ideal firing temperature, so follow the manufacturer's recommendations carefully. Use a pyrometer or kiln sitter to monitor the kiln's temperature throughout the firing process, and always allow pieces to cool slowly to avoid thermal shock or cracking.

4. Understanding Firing Atmospheres:

The atmosphere inside the kiln (oxidation or reduction) can affect the final appearance of your glaze. Oxidation firing occurs in kilns where plenty of oxygen is present, resulting in bright and vibrant colors. Reduction firing, on the other hand, involves limiting oxygen, which can create earthy or metallic finishes.

FAQs: Understanding Glazes, Firing Schedules, and Safe Handling of Materials

Pottery glazing and firing can seem complex, but with a little understanding of the processes involved, you'll gain confidence in creating beautiful, functional pieces. Here are answers to some frequently asked questions:

1. What Are Glazes and How Do They Work?

Glazes are liquid suspensions of finely ground minerals applied to pottery pieces before the glaze firing. When fired, these minerals melt and form a glass-like coating. Glazes can provide color, texture, and waterproofing to your pottery, and they come in a variety of finishes, including matte, glossy, and satin.

2.   What Firing Schedule Should I Follow?

The firing schedule depends on the clay body and glaze you're using. Typically, bisque firing is done at lower temperatures (around 1,800°F to 1,900°F or cone 06-04), while glaze firing happens at higher temperatures (2,100°F to 2,300°F or cone 6-10). Always consult the manufacturer's guidelines for the specific clay and glaze you are using.

3.   How Can I Safely Handle Pottery Materials?

Some materials used in pottery, particularly glazes, can contain toxic elements like lead or cadmium, especially in low-fire glazes. Always wear gloves and a dust mask when handling powdered glazes or clay to avoid inhalation. Proper ventilation is also important when firing the kiln to prevent exposure to harmful gases released during the process.

4. How Can I Avoid Glaze Defects?

Glaze defects like crawling, pinholing, and crazing can occur due to improper application or firing. To prevent crawling (where glaze pulls away from the surface), apply the glaze in even coats and make sure the bisque-fired piece is clean before glazing. For pinholes, ensure the clay body is free of impurities, and for crazing (fine cracks in the glaze), ensure that the glaze and clay body have compatible expansion rates.

By understanding these common concerns and addressing them proactively, you'll be able to tackle challenges with confidence and enjoy the art of pottery making to its fullest potential. Happy potting!

THE END

Made in United States
North Haven, CT
02 May 2025